Own Your Share of America

A Beginners Guide to Building Wealth through
Stock and Real Estate Investing

By Jerry Diorio – Real Estate Broker & Investor

TABLE OF CONTENTS

FORWARD - IF I KNEW THEN WHAT I KNOW NOW............4

CHAPTER 1 - GETTING YOUR FINANCIAL HOUSE IN ORDER 6

CHAPTER 2 - PLANNING FOR RETIREMENT.......................10

CHAPTER 3 - THE TEN PERCENT PRINCIPLE.......................17

CHAPTER 4 - GETTING STARTED WITH ASSOCIATIONS.25

CHAPTER 5 - A GUIDE THROUGH DIVIDEND REINVESTMENT PLANS 27

CHAPTER 6 - CHOOSING THE RIGHT STOCKS 37

CHAPTER 7 - INVESTMENT PROPERTY 101: HOW TO FIND, HOLD, AND BUILD WEALTH IN REAL ESTATE 39

CHAPTER 8 - BE A TEACHER.................................47

FORWARD

IF I KNEW THEN WHAT I KNOW NOW

You are now reading a book I hope will give you a good foundation on the road to your financial independence.

This book is based on solid principles that have been used for many years by thousands of investors to build their wealth.

Most of you are employed and earn a decent living, but somehow don't feel like you're getting ahead. That's because there are leaks in your bucket! Think about it! Your income is liquid. It gets put into your checking account - the Bucket. There are a lot of holes in that bucket that you don't realize and those holes don't pay you back.

We all start out in different financial positions after High School or College depending on what our parents taught us about money growing up. While making money during these early years in summer jobs, and even in jobs in our twenties we don't really think too far ahead. However, some of us learn in our early to late 20's (hopefully earlier) about making our money work for us, by putting a little aside each week and saving. The statement at the beginning of this paragraph I have heard time and time again from my Parents and Grandparents; "If I knew then what I know now". Regardless of your income or situation, it's never too late to start.

Savings is only part of it. There are two parts to life's financial equation. One is the Income side and the second is Expense side. If you are just starting out in life you're probably focused on the income side. If you are not, there probably have been times where you focused on the expense. The fact is that attention must always be made on the expense side. Every dollar should have a name, every month.

CHAPTER 1

GETTING YOUR FINANCIAL
HOUSE IN ORDER

Before you can invest in anything, you will need to figure out where your money is going now. Here are some tips for cutting expenses and get your financial house in order.

Let's first examine some basic expenses I call the "Four Necessities." The Four Necessities are your basics such as food, shelter (including utilities) basic clothing and transportation. So cut out the brand-name clothes, the fancy restaurants and even the expensive cable package. Just focus on these four necessities.

By maintaining the Four Necessities, you stabilize your living situation so you can begin to find margin in your budget to attack your debt or if you have no debt, start investing.

Remember this: Your creditors don't care about you. They just want to get your money. So focus on the important over the urgent. And that starts with taking care of your Four Necessities first.

Cut out extra expenses

Fortunately, most of you are healthy, productive individuals who should start doing something for yourself that you used to pay others to do, such as lawn maintenance, car washing, and yes, your laundry.

When I was single and worked in Manhattan, I didn't want to be bothered washing and ironing my own dress shirts. Back in the 80's I would pay $1.10 to $1.50 per shirt, times 5 per week times approximately 50 weeks a year. Also, if you have Cable TV, cut the cord, put an antenna on your house and go with Netflix or another service like Hulu. Every little bit helps!

Analyse your priorities.

If you're driving an expensive car, sell it and buy one that more fits your income ratio. If you're making $30K a year and your new car was $15K, you can't afford it! You will also save on insurance and your payments will be a lot less. If you are in the market for a car, consider a used or "pre-owned" car. Remember, everyone drives a used car!

If you have any habits like drinking alcohol or smoking, quit! Think of all the money you will save and you may live longer to spend it, too. I figured out how much the average smoker spends on smoking each year. If a smoker buys a carton per week, costing $110.00, that person is spending $5720.00 per year. Poof! This is one habit no one needs!

I am sure the ladies have some expenses you would rather forget, such as excessive spending on clothes, jewellery, shoes, make-up, and accessories. Also on manicures, pedicures and the hair salons! Think about that. Is all that expense absolutely necessary? Try doing some of these tasks yourself and you will be amazed how much you save.

This brings me to coupons for groceries. I do the grocery shopping in our house. I have been a fan of coupons since I can remember. Last year, my coupon savings totalled over $800.00. You should also buy in bulk when there are sales, if you have the freezer or storage room and the extra cash to layout. This will dramatically decrease your weekly grocery bill.

Take charge of your debt

Tackle those Student Loans and Credit Card balances with the same gusto used to run up those bills by using the debt snowball method.

Here's how the Debt Snowball Method Works. The debt snowball method is a debt reduction strategy where you pay off debts in order of smallest to largest, gaining momentum as each balance is paid off. When the smallest debt is paid in full, you roll the money you *were* paying on that debt into the next smallest balance.

It looks something like this:

Step 1: List your debts from smallest to largest.
Step 2: Make minimum payments on all your debts except the smallest.
Step 3: Pay as much as possible on your smallest debt.
Step 4: Repeat until each debt is paid in full.

Develop a zero based budget to give every dollar a name. If you have to, get a second job or other source of income to grow your snowball.

CHAPTER 2

PLANNING FOR RETIREMENT

Many individuals harbour rosy misconceptions about how much income and/or assets they would need to become financially independent and live a comfortable retirement.

Today, pension and Social Security benefits are not what they once were, financial institutions and insurance companies have become a concern and require close scrutiny, and health care costs seem to be rising out of control. With all of these scenarios continuing to be played out, wise planning is essential.

It is important that you do not get caught up in myths about achieving financial freedom and instead base your own retirement and financial independence planning upon solid facts. A look at the popular myths and why they are myths should help keep you on the right track.

Myth 1: You will not need as much money during retirement as you do now.

The general rule of thumb says that you will need approximately 70% of your pre-retirement income to maintain a lifestyle similar to your current one. This may be true if you live your current lifestyle.

However, when you retire, you will have more free time for travel, leisure activities, hobbies, and other things you might like to do during your retirement years. All of these may mean an increased expense in these areas. In addition, medical expenses will increase at a faster rate than they likely did during your pre-retirement years. Also, your overall tax rate may not drop very much and you may live longer than you think. Currently, if you are age 65 your life expectancy is approximately 21 years, which is a good target to plan for depending on your situation. Finally, why plan for a meager retirement when you can begin planning well ahead and have the income you need to live the lifestyle you wish during retirement?

Myth 2: You can afford to start planning for your retirement a few years before your retirement date.

In fact, it is never too soon to begin planning for your retirement time is one of the most powerful tools in the accumulation of wealth. The sooner you start to accumulate assets and plan for your retirement years, the better, and the less you will need to set aside each year in order to reach your goals.

In order to achieve your various financial objectives, you need to have an active savings and investment program. Planning for your financial independence will require some thought and soul-searching analysis to determine what is really important to you since, for most of us, this will mean giving up some objectives in order to achieve others.

You should start to discuss and set specific goals for your financial independence at least 25 years ahead of time. You can always adjust each year for your objectives if necessary, but it is better to begin planning early than to wait.

Myth 3: Social Security will provide enough income for my retirement years.

The fact is that Social Security accounted for approximately 38% of the average retiree's' income in calendar year 1990. In 2016, the average benefit for all retired persons was approximately $1360 per month, even though the maximum monthly benefit was much higher. Although increases in benefits have occurred and may continue to occur, it is likely they may become less generous than they have in the past.

In addition, the current plans are to extend the age that you must reach in order to receive full retirement benefits. Thus, it is becoming ever more important for you to accumulate your own funds in addition to whatever the government programs can provide. Social Security should be considered a supplemental benefit to your retirement financial planning and not the foundation on which it is built.

Myth 4: I have my pension plan to provide for my retirement income and will not need any additional savings.

The truth is that without planning well in advance, it will be difficult to tell whether your pension, combined with Social Security, will or will not achieve your financial objectives.

If you are at a company that offers a defined benefit plan, your retirement benefit will be a monthly income stream based on some percentage of your salary during the last few years of your employment at the firm and the number of years you worked there. Just remember, most employees do not stay with one employer for a long period of time, and are unable to accumulate much in earned benefits.

In addition, many employers are replacing defined benefit plans with defined contribution plans and allowing employees more say in the management of these funds. It will be increasingly important for you to make the proper investment decisions if you are to achieve the accumulation level you need in order to live the lifestyle you would like during your retirement years. Thus, you will see fewer employers committing to a monthly income stream for their retiree's in the future; instead, you will have employers making plans available and probably contributing a portion of the funds to a retirement account for individuals. However, it will be your job to see that the contributions accumulated are at rates sufficient for you to achieve your financial objectives and if they are not, to create your own supplemental savings plan in order to see that your objectives are achieved.

Myth 5: Medicare will take care of my health insurance.

Typically, Medicare pays less than half of a retiree's medical bills, and you usually cannot start collecting this until age 65. In addition, many employers are cutting back on medical coverage for retiree's due to the cost. You will need to look at and plan for the costs involved for your health insurance during the retirement years and consider Medicare supplements and possibly long-term care insurance coverage. For many of us, these are costs that we never had, or incurred minimally, during our working years but which will now be a major part of our annual budget.

Myth 6: All of my assets are in safe vehicles for long-term accumulation and do not need to be watched closely.

The fact is that all investments need to be watched. With the banking and savings and loan crisis along with the recent concerns over insurance companies, the "old stand-bys," which were once considered our safe havens, have come into question.

In addition, the practice of putting all of our assets into extremely safe vehicles brings to bear an additional risk-loss of purchasing power. The loss of purchasing power can be a devastating risk to deal with because it happens gradually over a long period of time, and many times goes unnoticed year to year. The only thing you know is that things seem to get a little bit tighter each year, but you still try to make it. By the time you realize you need to make major adjustments, it is almost too late.

Myth 7: You can always use the equity in your home to add to your retirement via a reverse mortgage.

While it is possible that you could make the above scenario happen, it is unlikely that this will add much to your retirement income, especially without making you extremely uncomfortable, not to mention a really bad idea.

Over the last few years since the crash, in many areas of the country home prices have continue to drop. It is unclear whether home prices will bounce back and increase with inflation, as they did in years past. In addition, other costs to maintain your home such as property taxes, repair costs, etc., will tend to increase.

If you do use your home to supplement your retirement income, sell it and remember to take advantage of all the tax breaks available to you, especially when downsizing.

Myth 8: If need be, my family could always help me out.

The fact is that many of us may use this as an excuse for delaying our retirement planning but, in reality, no one wants to rely on other family members to help them financially fund their retirement years.

If anything, these are the years when you want true financial independence and do not want to feel as if you are a burden on your family. This independence becomes more and more important as 'you reach your retirement years, and anyone using the above statement to rationalize away their need for savings and retirement planning will live to regret it!

Myth 9: Money is everything when it comes to retirement planning.

Nothing could be further from the truth! While money is important, it is the lifestyle decisions that are really the most important concerns for your retirement years.

Money is important in that it is needed in order to finance the lifestyle decisions you make, and for this reason it is important to plan as early as possible for funding the lifestyle you would like to lead.

Where you live, how and where you will vacation, what you will do with your spare time, and a realization of your participation in other interests all become extremely important issues during your retirement years.

You may even decide to use your mortgage-free real estate investments to replace your working income and retire earlier than thought possible. You could start a second business or make one of your hobbies or interests your remaining life's work. The whole point here is that a comfortable and successful retirement is about fulfilment of objectives and not accumulation of money. It is about enjoying your life to the fullest, which is based on your definition of happiness. Money is a tool to help you achieve these ends, but it is not the end itself. As you think about some of the issues presented here, ask yourself whether or not you are basing your own financial independence upon any of these "myths." If so, it is time to take a serious look at your financial independence planning and get on track so that your retirement years can be lived to their fullest in the manner you wish and not be constrained by the mistakes you made in previous years.

CHAPTER 3

THE TEN PERCENT PRINCIPLE

I started my career as a printer in 1987, growing my business into a Marketing Agency after 23 years in business. Eight years ago I sold that business and started a new venture as a Real Estate Broker. In addition, I have been a real estate investor since the late 90's.

I realized way back in the early 90's that I knew nothing about financial planning, and it was time to learn.

One Saturday, we were invited to a family barbeque at my Aunt Bev and Uncle Bob's. I explained my situation to my Uncle Bob. I told him what we wanted to achieve. "Is it possible?" I asked.

"He told me, true wealth is possible if you follow one simple principle: Invest ten percent of all you make for long-term growth. If you follow that one simple principle, someday you will be very wealthy."

"That's all?" I asked. "Patience, he said." I wasn't very impressed when my Uncle Bob told me this. My household budget was already designed to save even more than ten percent and, at that point, it wasn't working and I was far from wealthy.

But, Uncle Bob continued to explain a few things that turn a simple principle into an extremely powerful thought.

"Jerry, if you invested twenty-four hundred dollars a year, say two hundred dollars a month, for the next thirty years, and averaged a fifteen percent return per year, how much money do you think you would have?" So I tried to calculate and he interrupted. "The answer is one point four million dollars." I could not believe it! Uncle Bob went on, " If you had started putting thirty dollars a month away, at age eighteen and you continued until age sixty-five, averaging fifteen percent annual return, how much money would you end up with?"

I just smiled this time. He continued, "The answer is two million six hundred and seventy-nine thousand dollars." Uncle Bob continued, "Twenty two years ago, I started my savings with thirty dollars a month, which was approximately ten percent of my earnings. I have achieved just under a fifteen percent average annual return. In addition, as my income rose, my ten percent saving principle rose accordingly. Thirty dollars a month became sixty dollars, then a hundred, and eventually hundreds of dollars a month. You are looking at a very wealthy man!"

I could not believe it. My uncle a wealthy man? He continued, "Remember that your wages will continue to rise too, as will your ten percent savings. My original ten percent stake was only thirty dollars a month; yours will be much more, and so will your total wealth.

That will do a lot to offset inflation. If you handle your savings wisely, your growth rate should far exceed the inflation rate. Maybe not every year, but certainly on average."

Some of you are probably asking, how do I save ten percent of my gross income, when money keeps running out before the month does? It's simple. Pay yourself first!

I can't tell you what those three little words have meant to me. Although I am talking about the ten percent principle, the same holds true for all savings. Whether you are saving for a down payment, a car, a trip, whatever, the most effective thing is to have the money come right off your pay check, or right out of your bank - before you have a chance to spend it. Try it, and I guaranty after a few months, you won't even miss it!

I want to make something clear here. At different times in your life, you're going to have to save for various things - a house, a car, a trip, whatever. A house in particular, is a major expenditure. There is no way to achieve some goals without sacrificing by cutting back on unnecessary expenses or increasing your income. But the ten percent principle of savings is different. It's regular. It's constant. You don't even see it. It comes right off your pay check or out of your bank. You won't believe how easy that makes it.

The sky is falling!

Despite all the whining and all the predictions of doom and gloom, times are good and, thinking "long term" they will

19

continue to get better. Like DVRs, iPads and self-parking cars, our parents didn't enjoy technology like that when they were young. The fact is we are living in great times. If you're healthy and living in the United States, you have little to complain about, apart from the New York Giants coaching staff!

I know we have huge deficits, major national healthcare problems and so on. And these are serious problems. Unfortunately, we will always have serious problems. However, equating serious with fatal would be to greatly underestimate this country.

'It is a gloomy moment in history ... never has the future seemed so dark and incalculable. The United States is beset with racial, industrial and commercial chaos, drifting we know not where. Of our troubles, no man can see the end.' Quite an editorial, don't you think? It was written in Harper's Magazine in 1847!

I believe that the next ten to twenty years will present some of the greatest opportunities ever to Own Your Share of America. So much change, so many things happening. The only way to be a part of it all and to share in the successes is through ownership.

Dollar cost averaging

Market fluctuations are like a roller coaster, they're fun on the way up, but scary on the way down. But, thanks to dollar cost averaging, even downside fluctuations can work to your advantage.

Dollar cost averaging is as close to infallible investing as you can get. It slants the odds in an investor's favour, yet I've read all kinds of financial planning books that haven't even mentioned it. Because you're putting in a fixed amount each month, you obtain more shares at the lower prices. If you bought twenty shares at five dollars, but only ten shares at ten dollars, it means that your average cost per share will be lower than the average price per share. In the long run, or even in the short run, that bodes well for the investor. Dollar cost averaging is great stuff! Here is an example:

Let's say an investor invests $1,000 on the first of each month into Mutual Fund XYZ. Assume that over a period of five months, the share price of Mutual Fund XYZ on the beginning of each month was as follows:

• Month 1: $20

• Month 2: $16

• Month 3: $12

• Month 4: $17

• Month 5: $23

On the first of each month, by investing $1,000, the investor can buy a number of shares equal to $1,000 divided by the share price. In this example, the number of shares purchased each month is equal to:

• Month 1 shares = $1,000 / $20 = 50

• Month 2 shares = $1,000 / $16 = 62.5

- Month 3 shares = $1,000 / $12 = 83.33
- Month 4 shares = $1,000 / $17 = 58.82
- Month 5 shares = $1,000 / $23 = 43.48

Regardless of how many shares the $1,000 monthly investment purchased, the total number of shares the investor owns is 298.14, and the average price paid for each of those shares is $16.77. Considering the current price of the shares is $23, this means an original investment of $5,000 has turned into $6,857.11.

If the investor had invested all $5,000 on one of these days instead of spreading the investment across five months, the total profitability of the position would be higher or lower than $6,857.11 depending on the month chosen for the investment. However, no one can time the market. DCA is a safe strategy to ensure an overall favorable average price per share.

Equity Oriented Mutual Funds

Simply stated, a mutual fund is a professionally managed pool of money. The pool is made up of money from people like you and me, people numbering in the thousands. We all put our money together and hand in over to someone who knows, or supposedly knows, what he or she is doing. There are all sorts of benefits. Most important is the one I just mentioned: professional money management.

Second, mutual give you diversification. Most people don't have enough money to buy a properly diversified portfolio, with stocks in different industries. By pooling resources, individuals can gain a pro-rata share in a vast array of securities. Hence the saying, don't put all your eggs in one basket.

Third, mutual funds are hands off investment. There is no ongoing research and decision making process of the investor. This feature is very important, because some of you don't have the time to look after your investments. With mutual funds, that isn't a problem. They have a low PITA factor. What's a PITA Factor? Pain in the Ass factor ... a highly technical investment term.

But, they are subject to risk. There are no guarantees, and they do fluctuate up and down. If your professional money manager makes a series of bad investment decisions, they will be reflected in the performance of the fund. The key to any mutual fund is its manager. You're buying professional money management, so be sure to read up on the manager before investing with a particular fund. Money magazine does a great job monitoring performance and highlighting industry leaders. Keep an eye out for Money's once a year issue on mutual funds.

Always remember this one word; timing. If you buy a common stock fund at the height of the market, you're asking for trouble. 'Buy low, sell high' has long been a cliché' of the investment business, but truer words have never been spoken. If you rush in and buy a fund, or for that matter any investment, because your friend's has tripled in the last five years, you're probably making a mistake. It's when your friend's investment has gone down thirty percent over the last two years that you're probably looking at a good time to buy. Mutual funds are a seven to ten year investment, because they are hard to time and they do fluctuate, so you have to be thinking long term.

CHAPTER 4

GETTING STARTED WITH ASSOCIATIONS

Do you like stock investing but want more of hands-on approach? I have found that joining The National Association of Investors Corporation (NAIC) now called Better Investing, to be very helpful in investment education and get you started fast. Membership benefits include Better Investing Magazine. The magazine for the individual investor. Each month articles include "Stock to Study," "Undervalued Stock," "Beginners Comer" and "Repair Shop" along with many other wealth building, portfolio management and investment education features. The Low Cost Investment Plan lets you build a portfolio on a shoestring. Your first purchase is just one share of stock in the company of your choice. Then on a regular basis you send in additional money to the company and it's invested in the stock for you, with dividends reinvested in more stock. Currently, there are more than 800 companies participating in the low cost plan.

Since 1951, Better Investing's publications and educational resources have enabled millions of everyday people from all walks of life to take control of their own investments and make more informed financial decisions.

Another Association is the American Association of Individual Investors. It was founded in 1978 to assist individuals in becoming effective managers of their own investments. They offer the AAII Journal, which is the primary benefit of membership. It is published 10 times a year and focuses on providing information and how-to articles that help the individual learn investment fundamentals. The Journal does not promote a specific viewpoint or recommends specific investments, and it does not accept advertising.

CHAPTER 5

A GUIDE THROUGH DIVIDEND REINVESTMENT PLANS

Over 800 companies in the U.S. offer dividend reinvestment plans to their shareholders and are listed in the AAll Journal's Individual Investor's Guide to Dividend Reinvestment Plans, with NAIC's Better Investing Magazine and other DRIP Directories.

Dividend reinvestment plans are custom-made for long-term buy-and-hold investors. While they are not on their own a reason to buy a stock, they serve as a share- holder bonus on a company with promising long-term growth prospects.

The concept is straightforward: Instead of sending participating investors cash dividends, the company applies those dividends to the purchase of additional company shares.

There are several advantages to investors who participate: Dividend payments are put to work, transaction costs are eliminated or held to a minimum, and the additional shares are purchased gradually over time an easy-to-implement form of dollar cost averaging.

Various features make certain plans even more attractive. They include:

1. Optional cash payments that allow participants to purchase additional shares through the plan.

2. Partial reinvestment of dividends, allowing participants to receive cash dividends on some of their shares while reinvesting dividends on the remaining.

3. Automatic investments through an investor's checking account.

4. IRA accounts that allow participants to invest tax-deferred savings in the plan.

5. Discounts on the price of shares purchased through the plan.

6. Service fees and brokerage costs for share purchases that are picked up by the company rather than the participants.

How do you join?

Most dividend reinvestment plans require that you own at least one share (and sometimes more) registered in your name you are a shareholder of record. That means your name appears on the corporate records as the owner of the shares rather than the nominee name (street name) of the broker or bank that may have purchased the shares for you (and who may be safekeeping them for you). If your shares are held in street name, you should ask your broker to transfer the shares to your own name.

A small number of companies will sell initial shares directly to investors, so no purchases need to be made through a broker.

Usually, a company will send you a dividend reinvestment plan prospectus or description and an authorization card once you become a registered shareholder. You can also call the company (ask for shareholder relations) or the dividend reinvestment plan agent and request these items.

You should read the plan prospectus or description carefully. While the overall structure of most dividend reinvestment plans is similar, they vary in the details. The prospectus or description will provide information on such items as: eligibility requirements, plan options, costs, how and when purchases are made, how and when certificates will be issued, and how participants withdraw.

How they work

Dividend reinvestment plans are part of a company's overall shareholder relations effort and primarily serve existing shareholders.

Some companies' utilities in particular have extensive investor relations departments and administer their own dividend reinvestment plans. Most companies, however, appoint an outside agent to serve as the administrator for the plan.

The agent also is responsible for the purchase of company shares for the plan. When you join a plan, you will sign a card that authorizes the agent to make purchases on your behalf.

Shares purchased under a dividend reinvestment plan are held by the plan and registered in the nominee name of the agent or plan trustee on behalf of the participants, each of whom has an account under the plan. For most participants, that means you will hold the company's shares in two places your original registered shares, with the certificates either held by you or in custody at a bank or brokerage firm, and the shares purchased through the dividend reinvestment plan, held by the plan.

The administrator maintains records, sends account statements to participants, furnishes certificates for shares upon request and liquidates participants' shares when they leave the plan. The agent also is responsible for the purchase of company shares for the plan. When you join a plan, you will sign a card that authorizes the agent to make purchases on your behalf.

Many plans will allow participants to deposit certificates of shares registered in their own name into their dividend reinvestment plan account for safekeeping at no charge or for a modest fee; these shares are then treated in the same way as the other shares in the participant's account. Thus, it is possible to consolidate your shares in one safe location.

Certificates for shares purchased under the plan are usually issued only upon writ- ten request, although often at no charge. Certificates are also issued when a participant no longer wants to participate in the plan.

Companies with different classes of shares outstanding may allow shareowners of several forms to participate. Sometimes, reinvestment is in stock of the same form for instance, preferred reinvests in preferred; sometimes it is all reinvested into one form for instance, all reinvestment is in common stock. Check the prospectus to make sure you know where your dividends are being reinvested.

Plan Options

The basic plan offers reinvestment of dividends on all shares of stock registered in the participant's name. This is often referred to as full reinvestment.

Under some plans, it isn't necessary to reinvest all dividends. Instead, participants are allowed to reinvest dividends on a portion of their registered shares while receiving cash dividends on the remaining shares. This is usually referred to as a partial reinvestment option.

Many plans allow participants to purchase additional shares by making cash payments directly to the plan. This option is often referred to as optional cash payment, and since the allowable amounts can be large, it offers participants a low-cost way to build a sizeable holding in a company. The payments are optional participants are not committed to making periodic cash investments. However, usually there are minimums for each payment made, and often there is a maximum. It is also important to note the frequency with which the plan invests cash payments, since interest is not paid on payments received in advance of actual investment.

There is a twist on the cash payment option. Some companies will allow registered shareholders to make cash investments without requiring them to reinvest dividends on the shares they are holding, although they may do so if they want. This is frequently referred to as the cash payment only option. An added convenience for participants who wish to make systematic cash investments is an automatic investment feature that is offered by many companies. The company or the plan agent automatically debits the investor's checking or savings account at regular intervals to purchase additional shares.

Full reinvestment and the partial reinvestment option concern dividends on shares registered in the participant's name. What about dividends paid on shares that are purchased and held in the plan? Under most but not all dividend reinvestment plans, dividends paid on these shares are automatically reinvested.

The Costs

The cost of participating in a dividend reinvestment plan is low, particularly compared to the alternative of going through a broker. Participant costs usually come in two forms: service charges and prorated brokerage commissions. Service charges cover administrative costs and are generally levied on each transaction; participants can hold costs down by combining a cash payment with a dividend reinvestment transaction, since usually the charges are capped.

Brokerage commissions levied on open market shares are at institutional rates (since the number of shares purchased is large), and are therefore considerably lower than the rate an investor would pay on his own.

Many companies cover all of the costs for share purchases from both reinvested dividends and optional cash payments. Some companies levy service charges, others pro- rate brokerage costs, still others charge participants for both there are many variations, so check the prospectus or plan description carefully.

When participation is terminated, some dividend reinvestment plans will sell plan shares for you if you prefer, instead of sending you certificates. The cost to the participant is usually any prorated brokerage commissions, a lower-cost alternative than selling through a broker. Some plans will sell plan shares for you even if you are not terminating. Check the prospectus or plan description.

Share Purchases

The source of share purchases under a dividend reinvestment plan is spelled out in the plan description and prospectus.

The most common source is the secondary market through a securities exchange where the shares are traded or in the over-the-counter market, or through negotiated transactions.

Another source for some is the company itself, using authorized but unissued shares of common stock or shares held in the company's treasury.

In plans that prorate brokerage commissions among participants, the source of share purchases is a concern. When shares are purchased directly from the company, there are no brokerage expenses to prorate.

From the company's point of view, dividend reinvestment plans that purchase shares directly from the company provide an inexpensive source of financing. The proceeds often are used for general corporate purposes. On the other hand, from an investor's viewpoint new issues serve to dilute existing shares, which can depress share prices.

When does the agent buy shares? Investment dates are specified in the plan description or prospectus. Usually, they coincide with the dividend payment date, but many companies that allow participants to make cash investments have additional investment dates.

When shares are purchased in the secondary markets, share purchases begin but don't necessarily end on the investment date. Most plans give some discretion to the agent, since a large purchase on a single date could affect share price; usually, however, it is required that all monies be invested within 30 days. The share price for each participant is an average price of all shares purchased for that investment period.

When shares are purchased directly from the company, the prospectus will describe how the share price is determined. Usually, it is based on an average of the high and low or the closing price for the stock as reported by a specified source.

Some companies offer participants discounts on the share price, but there is wide variation on how this is offered. Most often, the discounts are available only on shares purchased with reinvested dividends, but sometimes, discounts apply to shares purchased both with reinvested dividends and with cash payments. And, a few companies offer dis-counts only on newly issued corporate shares, and not on shares that must be purchased in the secondary markets. Discounts are described in detail in the plan's prospectus.

Taxes?

Dividend reinvestment plans have many advantages, but their tax status unless you are investing through an IRA (offered by only a few companies) is not one of them. Whether you receive your dividends in cash or have it reinvested, a taxable event has occurred. In addition, if you reinvest dividends, the IRS considers the dividend to be equal to the fair market value of shares acquired with reinvested dividends. The fair market price is the price on the exchange or market where shares are traded, not any discounted price. Furthermore, any brokerage commissions paid by the company in open market purchases are considered additional dividend income to the participant.

When shares are sold, the tax basis is the fair market value as of the date the shares were acquired, plus any brokerage commissions paid by the company and treated as income to the participant.

Participants receive 1099-DIV forms each year from the company detailing dividends to be treated as income as reported to the IRS. Check with the plan directly.

CHAPTER 6

CHOOSING THE RIGHT STOCKS

There are three practical rules you can follow to limit risk and obtain strong investment results:

Avoid unnecessary risk: The primary avoidable risk is individual company or industry risk, which can be diversified away. While investors with computers can use sophisticated computer models to accomplish this, it is also effective to simply select a portfolio of at least 10 different stocks with no more than one or two in the same industry.

The other avoidable risk is bad judgment made in hasty research of the company, panicking in fast markets or deviating from set plans.

Invest in stocks for the long term: The long-term portfolio has two key characteristics: It has no dollars in it that you expect to need in less than four years, and all of the money has been put in gradually over at least two years and not all at once. It is the port-folio's commitment to stocks, and not to any individual stock, that should be long term. Individual stocks can be sold whenever a better opportunity (net of taxes and transaction costs) presents itself.

Choose stocks for their potential for high return: Focus on those characteristics that indicate the best possibility for growth, and not on defensive factors. These can be quantitative factors that have predicted growth in the past or qualitative factors such as the company's management, products or markets.

If you follow these rules, your portfolio value may fluctuate, but in the long run you should outperform most institutional portfolios.

For those of us without the time to do our own research, the NAIC offers a subscription to its Investor Advisory Service for $149.00 per year. I signed on for this service because I don't have the time to do my own research and I want to invest in companies that are judged to have a 3-1 probability of doubling in 5 years. The service offers completed Stock Selection Guides, all the stat and a description of the company. You are also informed of stocks you already are invested in, and they help you make sense out of economic developments so that you can make informed investment decisions.

CHAPTER 7

INVESTMENT PROPERTY 101: HOW TO FIND, HOLD, AND BUILD WEALTH IN REAL ESTATE

The fact is that no matter what the state the economy is in, everyone needs a place to live. That being said, my preferred method of investing is in real estate. There is nothing wrong with investing in both, but you have more control with real estate.

An investment property can range from a small condo rental all the way up to a skyscraper along the Manhattan skyline – and everything in between. So how do you know the best kind of investment property for you? Furthermore, how do you get involved in this game that has made so many people wealthy in the history of civilization?

This chapter is going to give you a crash course in choosing the best investment properties, financing that purchase, and ultimately building serious wealth through real estate investing.

What Classifies a Good Investment Property?

Before getting into the specifics of how to find and fund your investment property, I want to first take a step back and look at exactly what defines a good investment property? Sure, you could go and purchase any piece of real estate, but a true investment property is one that helps you build wealth, often through multiple streams.

A single investment property typically offers several different avenues to build wealth:

1. Appreciation: When property values rise, the difference between what you owe and what its worth will increase.

2. Cash Flow: When a property is rented for income, and there is more income coming in each month than expenses going out.

3. Tax Benefits: Owning investment properties can help offset income from other areas of your life (see your tax advisor for more information.)

4. Principle Reduction: If you carry a loan on the investment property, each month your amount owed decreases slightly. For example, if you buy a single family home with a thirty year mortgage, after thirty years the loan would be paid off (with the help of the tenants' monthly rent payments) and you'll own the property free-and-clear.

Investment properties can utilize any of the above four avenues, but an ideal investment property will utilize all four. Also, different investment types will focus more or less on different avenues.

Choosing Your Ideal Investment Property

There are literally hundreds of ways to make money in real estate but as a property investor, you don't need to do every one. In fact, it's often best to focus on just one property type and become a professional in that niche before trying something new.

A few of the more common investment types are:

- Single Family Homes

- Small Multifamily Properties (2-4 units)

- Apartment Complexes

- Commercial Buildings

- Mobile Homes

- And many, many more.

Finding The Perfect Property To Invest In

Once you've decided on the property type you want to invest in, the next step is searching that property out. There are numerous ways to find investment property, but the most common methods are:

- **The MLS:**

The MLS, or Multiple Listing Service, is a collection of lists put together by local real estate agents that include all the homes currently for sale through an agent. In the old days, agents kept their listings in a file cabinet, but today you can search the MLS online, through multiple websites like Realtor.com, Zillow.com, or Trulia.com. Buying a property through an MLS listing is as easy as finding a real estate agent you like (and trust) and letting them submit an offer for you. Typically, the MLS is used primarily for single family homes and small multifamily properties, though larger multifamily and commercial properties can sometimes be found as well.

- **Commercial Broker:**

Typically, if you are looking to buy commercial real estate, a commercial real estate broker will be a valuable member of your team. Often times, commercial brokers will have "pocket listings" which means deals that are not public knowledge. If commercial real estate is the niche you've chosen, definitely find a commercial broker you can trust.

- **Loopnet:**

Loopnet.com is the largest listing site for commercial and large multifamily properties. You can search for anything from a small apartment building to a office building or restaurant here.

- **Direct Mail**

Direct mail is the process of sending out a large number of letters or postcards to a targeted list of individuals, based on certain criteria. Lists can be obtained from many sources and may be cheaper than you think. Check out services like postcardmania.com or click2mail to learn more specifics on pricing and options. You may send out 1000 letters and only hear back from 50 people – but if you can close just one deal, it can often be a great way to buy directly from an owner before a real estate agent gets involved.

- **Networking**

Finally, many individuals find their ideal investment property simply by networking. Whether through formal networking channels like investment clubs or simply through person to person contact in daily life, many deals are exchanged through personal connections. Be sure to have a professional business card on you at all times – you never know when you may need it.

- **Funding Your Purchase**

You can easily fund your real estate purchases if you have the cash – but not everyone can simply do that. Additionally, those who can pay with all cash often choose not to, because they'd rather utilize the concept of "leverage" to control more property than an all-cash purchase would allow. This section is going to look at a few of the more common methods used to finance real estate.

- **Bank Loans:** If your credit and income are good, you can often fund your purchase through a bank, credit union, or mortgage broker. These rates are typically the lowest and are generally spread out over 15 to 30 years. You can check out current mortgage rates online or if you already have a relationship with a local lender, make the call and find out directly.

- **Hard Money Lenders:** If you only need the money for a short time (and plan to refinance or sell quickly,) hard money lenders can be a tool to use. Hard Money Lenders are short term lenders who look primarily at the deal, rather than the credit/income of the borrower. There are many risks and benefits to using hard money lenders, so be sure to research carefully. Google hard money lenders to find a directory online.

- **Self-Directed IRA** – Many people have IRA's, but few know that you can actually use your IRA to invest in real estate. Check with your tax advisor or financial planner to find out more about the rules for investing in real estate with your self-directed IRA.

- **Private Money:** With the low rates currently offered by most bank savings accounts and CDs, many wealthy individuals are turning to private lending to earn a higher rate. As an investor, you can often offer an individual a solid return, typically 8% - 12% secured by real estate, to the individual and use the money to fund your deals. Private lenders are typically known to the borrower (perhaps a family member or friend.)

- **Syndication:** As you progress in your real estate investing, you may find the need for larger sums of money than you could hope to generate alone. In these cases, real estate syndications are often formed to pool the money from multiple investors into a fund to invest in real estate. There are many laws concerning the forming of a syndication, so be sure to check with both your state and federal laws and consult with an attorney before forming a syndication.

Managing Your Purchase

After purchasing your property, the fun is not over. In fact, the decisions you make and the steps your take after your purchase can make your investment a solid one or a dud. Typically, there are two main choices when it comes to managing your property:

- **Self-Managed:** Many investors begin by managing your own properties. As a landlord, it is your responsibility to collect rent, enforce the lease, advertise and sign with new tenants, prepare or arrange maintenance, do the bookwork, and perform any and all other tasks as they occur. However, while most landlords typically begin doing everything themselves, many individual tasks (like plumbing) can actually be hired out to a professional for less than you think.

- **Property Management:** If you don't want to manage your own property, there are thousands of professional property management companies out there that can manage for you. If you choose to hire a manager, don't believe your investment is now 100% hands off though! Typically, your job becomes "managing the manager" and ensuring they are doing their job.

Your Next Steps

Buying an investment property is not a hobby – so don't treat it like one. Real estate investing is a business like any other, in need of systems, plans, and effective handling to be successful. The most important step for YOU to take right now is the next step. Determine what needs to happen next – and make it happen. Perhaps that means educating yourself further and jumping into the real estate forums online to ask a question. Perhaps that means calling up your real estate agent and start looking at properties.

Whatever your next step is, there is no better way to Own Your Share of America than through real estate.

CHAPTER 8

BE A TEACHER

Part of being an adult in our society understands how to use money wisely. And, as with other fundamental issues, it is best if one starts acquiring knowledge at a young age. Recognizing this, many parents wrestle with the issue of how to teach financial responsibility to their children, the task is a challenge in part because it is so difficult to get good sensible information about how to manage one's own money.

Consider the sources of information typically available to a young person growing up in our culture. Families, who often are reluctant to discuss money with their children; Social media, Movies and TV presents a fantasy land where financial limits and financial differences don't occur; Newspapers and magazines, which receive substantial advertising revenue from companies promoting an array of often confusing products in advertisements that purport to impart investment information;

The government, which doesn't do much to advertise tax rates, but does have active advertising campaigns for lotteries;

Hearsay, which tends to focus on those extraordinary, mythical-sized portfolio gains rather than on the down-to-earth stuff that works. Who would ever brag about living within their income, or saving regularly? And the apparent "good life," led by people, who like our government, are living over their income.

While appearances are enticing, the harsh financial realities of high debt and of meager savings for retirement are not visible to a young person looking around for clues about how the world works. All a young person sees are the fancy clothes, the expensive cars, and the big house. In light of this, how can financial management skills be instilled across the generations?

According to educators, learning about money not only happens best when exposure starts early, but also when responsibility comes in steadily increasing, age-appropriate steps. In other words, kids need to have the real world of financial limits, choices, and consequences made visible and accessible to them from an early age, in ever-larger doses.

At younger ages, it is important to have lots of hands-on experiences. By about age four, kids are ripe for learning about the world beyond them, especially handling transactions, contributing to family outings, and noticing different jobs in the community.

Upper-elementary-age kids are ready to have responsibility that increases slowly but steadily; they need to make a lot of mistakes. Teenagers and young adults are ready to consolidate the earlier experience of knowing what money can buy and how to make choices, and thus gain a sense of empowerment, control, and self-esteem.

At all stages, the process is important: It's worth the time and effort to let children come to their own decisions, and it's not only OK, but useful for them to make mistakes. Throughout this steadily increasing experience with money, kids can also benefit from opportunities to compare experiences with people in other generations. These opportunities to compare experiences can open up refreshingly frank conversations about a family's values.

How can any individual make use of these sensible but highly theoretical views? While there is plenty of financial illiteracy throughout the land, there are also many families who are successfully and happily transmitting habits of sound financial management to their children.

TIME TO GET GOING

The vehicle you choose to invest for building wealth is a personal choice, but it's important to just get started. Don't wait! Just start; write your plan, build your budget and think big!

God Speed and Good Fortune in Owning Your Share of America!

"Live, Love, Learn, Leave a Legacy"